SO-AVD-869

Fabulous Friendship Bracelets

This edition published in 2012
By SpiceBox™
12171 Horseshoe Way,
Richmond, BC, Canada V7A 4V4

First published in 2007
Copyright © SpiceBox™ 2007

All rights reserved.
No part of this book may be reproduced, stored in a retrieval system or transmitted in any form or by any means, electronic, mechanical, photocopying, recording or otherwise, without the prior written permission of the publishers and copyright holders.

ISBN 10: 1-926567-47-1
ISBN 13: 978-1-926567-47-1

CEO and Publisher: Ben Lotfi
Editorial: Trisha Pope
Creative Director: Garett Chan
Art Director: Christine Covert
Design & Layout: Morgen Matheson
Production: Mell D'Clute
Sourcing: Janny Lam
Photography: Garett Chan and James Badger
Special thanks to the models: Cristina Soares, Renee Lawless, Jorgina Thompson, Jamie Lacamell, Kelly Chan, and Claudia Chan

For more SpiceBox products and information, visit our website:
www.spicebox.ca

Manufactured in China

5 7 9 10 8 6 4

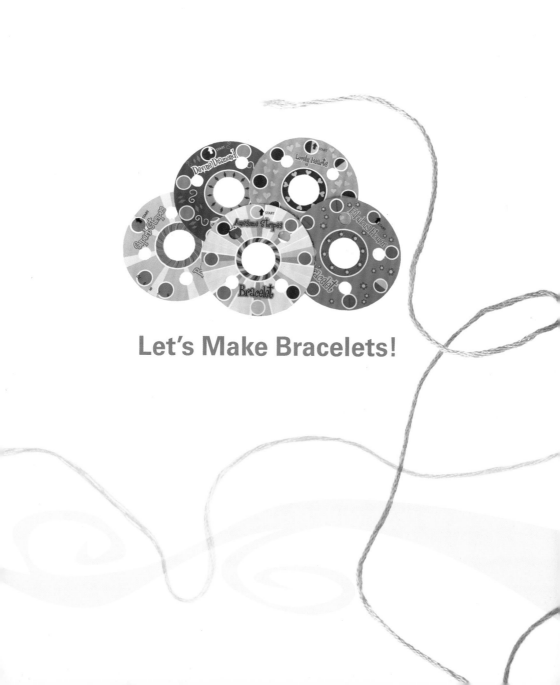

Let's Make Bracelets!

Table of Contents

Introduction

Friendship bracelets are a fun and simple craft to make, and this book and kit provides you with everything you will need to make dozens of these pretty accessories; plenty of threads and step-by-step instructions, as well as a really neat Friendship Wheel tool to help you create more complicated woven bracelets. Why not invite some of your friends over, and have a bracelet-making party? You can exchange them with each other, and then every time you look at the one tied on your wrist you will remember the stories and fun times you shared with your friends while you made them.

Friendship bracelets have a charming tradition to them that you should pass on when you give them away. Help fasten the bracelet onto your friend's wrist, and tell them to make a wish. When the bracelet is worn out and comes off their wrist, the wish will come true. But if they take it off themselves, they will have bad luck and the wish will not come true, so be careful!

Did you know: that once you accept a friendship bracelet from someone, you must wear it until it naturally wears out and falls off. If you take it off sooner than this, it means that you no longer want to be friends with the person who gave it to you!

Interesting Fact:
The origin of friendship bracelets is most likely Central American countries where they were a traditional handicraft. They only became popular in North America in the 1970s, but have remained popular ever since.

Getting Started

One of the things that has helped friendship bracelets maintain their popularity for more than thirty years is that you can achieve eye-catching results with very few supplies. Also, the techniques are straightforward and easy-to-learn.

You will first learn how to make the neat round friendship bracelets using the wheel that is in your kit. They are simple to make as long as you follow the pattern template and the instructions, and they are so cute! In addition to these bracelets, we also show you how to make the traditional friendship bracelets that are based on a series of knots. Patterns for the traditional bracelets start out from very basic ones that don't require any knotting, to ones that are quite complex. If you haven't ever made a friendship bracelet before, we recommend that you start right at the beginning with the very first bracelet and work your way through to the harder ones so that you learn each technique required in a logical order. But first, let's look at the materials in the kit as well as some basic instructions.

Materials and Techniques

The following materials will help you create cool friendship bracelets:

Threads: Embroidery thread is the most popular for friendship bracelets due to the wonderful array of colors that it is available in; it isn't, however, the only type of thread you can use. You could make a friendship bracelet with any lightweight yarns or string that will hold a knot, and there are lots of fun yarns you can find in a craft or hobby store to experiment with. Remember that the thicker the threads, the chunkier the bracelet will be.

Beads: Although none of the bracelets have directions specifically for adding beads to your bracelets, you can do this easily using your own sense of taste and style. You can either add beads to the ends so they dangle from your wrist, or slip them on to the threads as you are knotting. Use your own sense of fun to decide how to use the beads!

Safety Pins: The easiest way to secure the traditional style of knotted bracelets while you are working is to tape the end to your table or to pin the knot onto the leg of your jeans or to your bed.

Friendship Wheels and Templates: The Friendship Wheels in your kit comes in three pieces: the foam base, the template patterns and the clear disk. The foam base is notched all the way around, has four small holes, and one large one in the center. The holes in the templates need to line up with the holes in the wheel. Once they do, it can be secured into place by pressing the four knobs on the plastic disk into the holes snuggly to keep the template in place. Instructions for how to use the wheels are on pages 12-15.

The following techniques are important to know so that you can start and finish your bracelets properly each time.

Bracelet Length: To make your bracelet the correct length, measure your wrist with enough give so that the bracelet is a bit loose and will be comfortable on your wrist. Use the ruler on pages 58-63 to mark your measurements and your friends' measurements so that you always know how long to make your bracelets.

Starting your Bracelet: There are two ways to start your bracelet, either by leaving enough length to tie your bracelets onto your wrist (normally 2 inches/ 5 cm is enough) and then knotting the strings, or by folding your strings in half and tying a loop. Depending on which method you choose, you will need to cut different numbers of strings at different lengths. Each bracelet has a little chart to show how long your threads need to be, and how many to cut of each color.

Finishing your Bracelets: Once you have knotted the bracelets to the length you measured, you will need to tie the ends so they don't fall apart. If you have created a loop at the start of the bracelet, thread your loose ends through the loop and tie them into a knot around the loop. If you have left the ends of the threads long and tied a knot to start your bracelet, do the same to finish the bracelet and trim the ends so they are even. Then tie the bracelet on with the threads from both ends. You can then braid the ends, tie beads onto them, or trim them off..

The Friendship Bracelet Wheel

The Friendship Bracelet Wheel is the exciting, new way to make really terrific friendship bracelets. There are two wheels in the kit with interchangeable templates, so that you and your BFF can make them together and swap right away. In fact you will want to make plenty of these bracelets to give to your whole circle of friends, they are going to love them!

There are five different pattern templates you can use with the wheels and we have included two of each design in different color combinations. Use the colors the templates show to start, and then once you get the hang of it, experiment with your own color combinations.

Look at your pattern template and select the strings to match the colors on the tabs. Then, for each section on each tab, you will need one string in that color. Cut your strings 20 inches/ 50 cm long. Leave about 2 inches/ 5 cm at the end and then tie the strings into a knot.

OR

To tie a loop at the end, for every pair of same-colored tabs on the wheel, cut 1 string 40 inches/100 cm long. Fold the strings in half over a pencil or one of your fingers, and then tie the strings into a knot, pulling the knot tight up to the pencil. You should now have as many strings as the pattern requires in the correct colors.

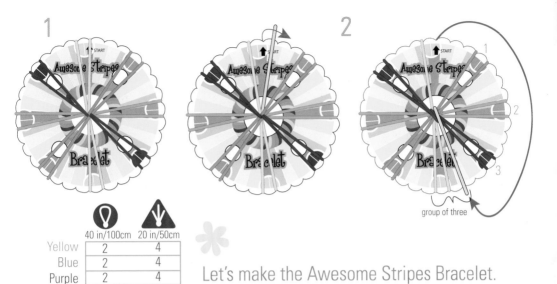

	![40 in/100cm icon] 40 in/100cm	![20 in/50cm icon] 20 in/50cm
Yellow	2	4
Blue	2	4
Purple	2	4
Red or Green	2	4

group of three

Let's make the Awesome Stripes Bracelet.

1. Start by either tying your threads into a loop or knot and center it in the middle of the hole in the wheel. Take one string at a time and notch it into the wheel where there is a tab that color. Position your wheel so the start arrow is at the top.

2. There will be two yellow strings notched into the wheel at the top. Unhook the right string, and rehook it into the wheel in the notch that is to the right of the yellow tab at the bottom of the wheel. Notice that you have a group of three strings now on the bottom of your wheel, and only one at the top.

3. Now, unhook the string on the left of the yellow tab at the bottom of the wheel, and rehook it into the notch at to the left of the single string in the yellow tab at the top.

4. Turn your wheel COUNTERCLOCKWISE, or to the LEFT one tab. The BLUE tab should now be at the top of the wheel.

5. Repeat steps 2-4, turning your wheel one tab at a time, and rehooking your strings, until your bracelet is long enough.

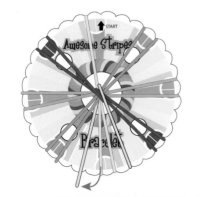

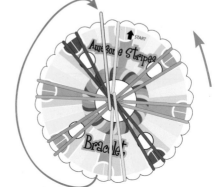

Divine Diamond

	40 in/100cm	20 in/50cm
Green or Orange	6	12
Purple or Blue	2	4

Follow the same instructions for the Awesome Stripes bracelet. This time, however, your top two notches will have purple strings. You will move the right string to the right of the green tab at the bottom of the wheel. You will then move the left string in the green tab to the left of the purple tab at the top.

Repeat the instructions in steps 2-5 above.

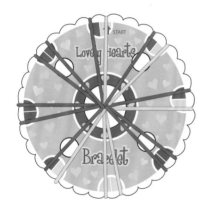

Lovely Hearts

	40 in/100cm	20 in/50cm
Yellow or Red	3	6
Purple or Mauve	5	10

This bracelet is a bit different because both sides of each tab are not always the same colors. However, don't get confused by this, follow exactly the same instructions for the Awesome Stripes and you will see a pretty bracelet of hearts emerge as you knot!

Fabulous Flower

	40 in/100cm	20 in/50cm
Yellow	n/a	1
Blue or Pink	n/a	6
Red or Blue	n/a	9

The single string creates the center of each flower, the 6 strings are the petals and the remaining 9 strings make up the background color. Once you have made this bracelet once to learn the pattern, choose your own colors and experiment to create different looks. Simply cut the same number of strings in different colors for each tab of the wheel and watch your flowers bloom!

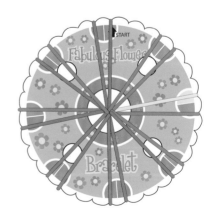

Hint: When taking a string off the top: take the thread from the right and replace on the right. When taking a string from the bottom: take from the left and return to the left.

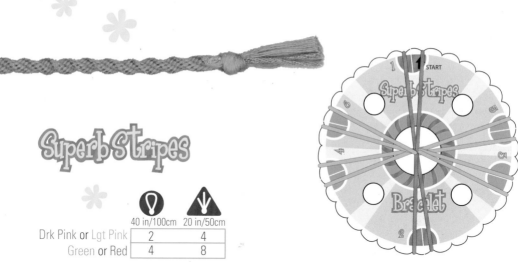

Superb Stripes

	40 in/100cm	20 in/50cm
Drk Pink or Lgt Pink	2	4
Green or Red	4	8

This pattern is a bit different because there are fewer strings and tabs and you are also not going to spin your wheel as you knot. Start your bracelet in the same way, by cutting and knotting your strings and then stringing them onto the wheel in the correct notches. Then, follow these instructions:

1. Unhook the TAB1 right string and move it to the right notch of TAB2
2. Unhook the left string of TAB2 and rehook it to the left of TAB1
3. Unhook the TAB3 right string and move it to the right notch of TAB4
4. Unhook the left string of TAB4 and rehook it to the left of TAB3
5. Unhook the TAB5 right string and move it to the right notch of TAB6
6. Unhook the left string of TAB6 and rehook it to the left of TAB5
7. Move each string CLOCKWISE - to the RIGHT, so that they are lined up on the tabs again.

Repeat steps 1-7 until your bracelet is long enough to tie on.

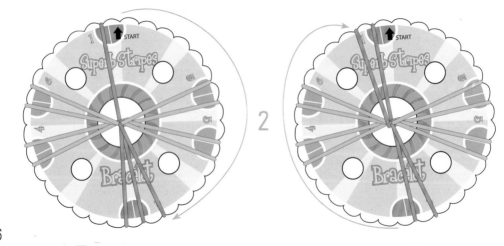

16

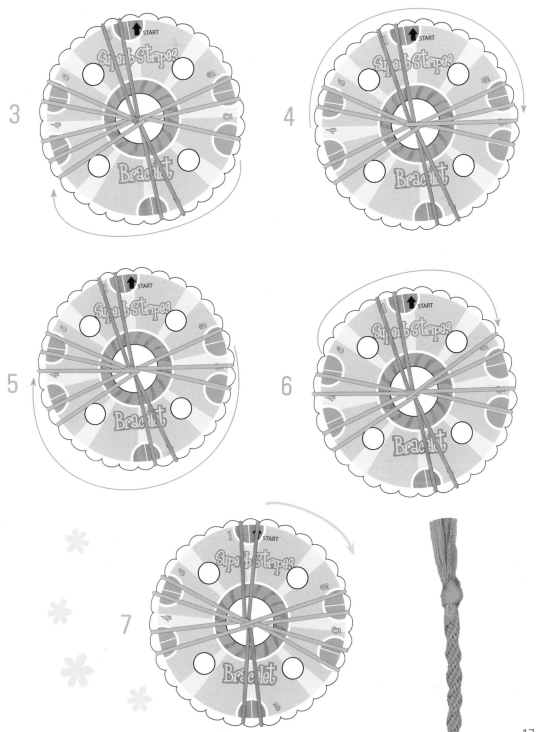

Traditional Style

Flat Friendship Bracelet styles

Variation: Cut three threads that are long enough to wrap around your waist two times. Using the same techniques, create a skinny belt for your waist that you can wear with shorts or jeans. Super stylish! You can also make it with more than three threads for a thicker twist.

The Twist

This bracelet doesn't require any knotting and can be made in a minute. You can wear it alone, but layering with other, more complicated bracelets looks great.

Tip: When you think you have twisted the threads enough, fold them in half to see how they wind together. If it looks too loose, unfold them and continue twisting some more!

1. Cut three colors of threads, each 24 inches / 60 cm long. Hold them together by one end and tie a knot about 3 inches / 8 cm from the top. Tape the knot to the table.

2. Hold the strings together and start twisting them together until they feel tight.

3. Hold the twist together with one hand and fold it in half around a finger on your other hand so that the ends of the threads meet at the top.

4. Keep holding the ends of the threads together at the top, and remove your finger from the middle of the twist. The threads should now quickly wind together, leaving a loop at the end.

5. Take the tape off the end of the bracelet, and tie the loose ends into a knot at the appropriate length. Slip both knotted ends through the loop of the bracelet to fasten it on your wrist.

2

3

(half way)

4

5

Variation: Try knotting beads onto the end of your braid, or even string some beads on to the threads as you are braiding for another hot look!

Beautiful Braid

Most of us have had a chance to create a braid, whether in a craft or with a friend's ponytail, but don't forget that you can make some pretty, simple bracelets by braiding as well.

N/A		16 in/40cm
		3 per color

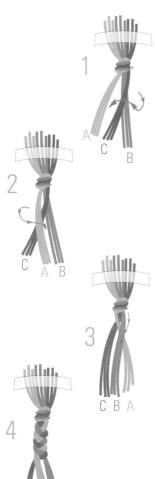

1. Spread out the three colors of strands. Pick up the right group of threads (C) and move them into the middle position as shown.

2. Now pick up the left group of threads (A) and move them into the middle position.

3. Pick up the threads that are now on the right (B) and move them into the middle position, and then repeat this with the left threads (C), moving them into the middle position.

4. Continue to repeat step 5 until you are finished, alternately moving the right threads and the left threads into the middle position of the braid until you have braided the complete length of the threads.

5. Knot the loose end and tie around your wrist. Easy!

A Basic Knot

In order to make a traditional, knotted friendship bracelet you need to tie a basic knot in two different directions.

A Left-loop Knot

1. Knot pieces of thread and tape them to a board. Hold the first string (1) firmly and cross the second string (2) over it leaving a loop like in the diagram.

2. Pass the second string (2) underneath the first string (1) and up through the loop — pull on it to make a knot. Slide the knot up to the top and pull it tight.

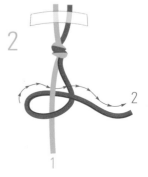

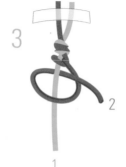

3. Now, repeat the process in order to make a double-knot. You've made your first complete left-loop knot!

A Right-loop Knot

1. Knot pieces of thread and tape them to a board. Hold the second string (2) firmly and cross the first string (1) over it, leaving a round loop made of the second string (2).

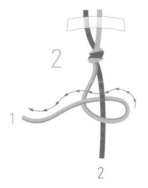

2. Send the first string (1) under the second string (2) and up through the loop. Softly pull on it to make a knot. Slide the knot up to the top of the board, and pull it tight.

3. Now, repeat the process in order to make a double-knot. You've made your first complete left-loop knot!

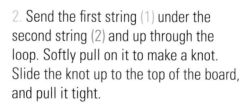

Hint: After tying a RIGHT LOOP KNOT, string 1 will lay on the RIGHT side of string 2. After tying a LEFT LOOP KNOT string 2 will lay on the LEFT of string 1.

Simple Stripes

Now it is time to start knotting! This is the most straightforward, knotted bracelet to make, as it only requires one type of knot that is repeated over and over. Work slowly until you get the rhythm of the knotting and then it will be a breeze to finish!

1. Choose six colors and cut one piece of each color, 28 inches/ 70 cm long. Tie a knot at the top and tape the knot to your work surface. Use the same colors of threads and organize them the way we do to make it easier to follow the instructions the first time.

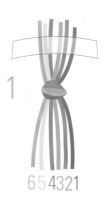

2. You are going to start using a LEFT LOOP KNOT (see page 22 to remember how to do this knot if you need to.) Pick up your right-most string, string 1, and tie a LEFT LOOP KNOT over string 2 beside it.

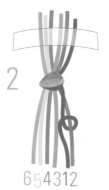

3. Using string 1 still, tie a LEFT LOOP KNOT over string 3.

4. Using string 1, tie a LEFT LOOP KNOT over string 4.

5. Using string 1, tie a LEFT LOOP KNOT over string 5.

6. Using string 1, tie a LEFT LOOP KNOT over string 6.

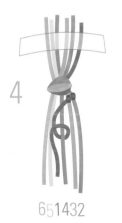

4

651432

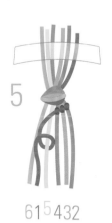

5

615432

6

165432

Hint: Don't forget, to make one complete LEFT LOOP KNOT you will tie the thread TWO times. See pages 22-23 to remind yourself if you need to!

Hint: This is a great bracelet to give to your guy friends. They will especially love it if you use the colors of their favorite sports team!

7. Now, pick up string 2, which is now the string on the far right. Using string 2, tie a LEFT LOOP KNOT over string 3.

8. Using string 2, tie a LEFT LOOP KNOT over string 4.

9. Using string 2, tie a LEFT LOOP KNOT over string 5.

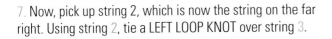

7

165423

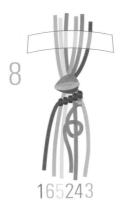

8

165243

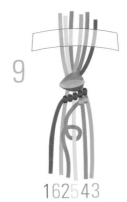

9

162543

26

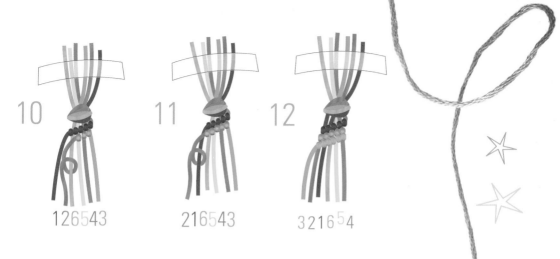

10
126543

11
216543

12
321654

10. Using string 2, tie a LEFT LOOP KNOT over string 6.

11. Using string 2, tie a LEFT LOOP KNOT over string 1, which is on the left hand side of the bracelet now. Do you see the pattern? You are creating stripes of knots across your bracelet.

You can probably guess the next steps, can't you?

12. Use string 3 to tie a LEFT LOOP KNOT on string 4, then string 5, then string 6, then string 1, then string 2.

13. Continue using the right-most string to tie LEFT LOOP KNOTS over each of the strings to the left of it until you have created the length of your bracelet.

14. Tie the loose ends into a knot, and tie on your bracelet!

Great job making your first knotted bracelet! Carry on through the book for other fun and exciting patterns.

Swirls

After all that knotting, here is a fun bracelet to try that has a different look to it; a row of knots swirls down the bracelet! It is just as straightforward, and the knots twist themselves around the bracelet naturally, as you go. Again, be patient and knot carefully for neat results. You want the knots to move from one color to the next without any gaps.

48 in/120 cm 1 per color	20 in/50 cm 2 per color

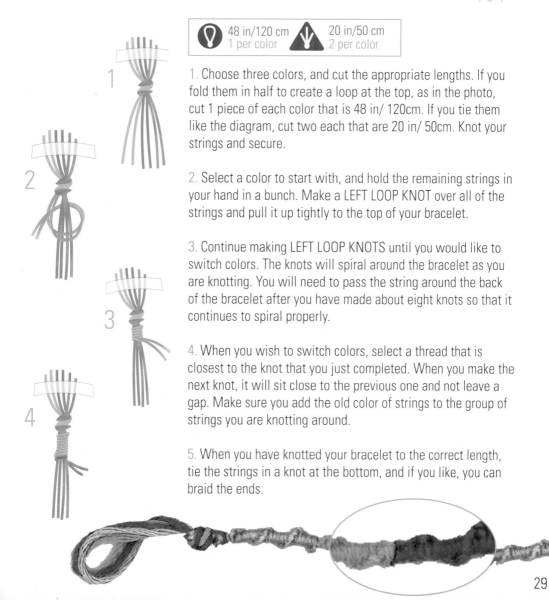

1. Choose three colors, and cut the appropriate lengths. If you fold them in half to create a loop at the top, as in the photo, cut 1 piece of each color that is 48 in/ 120cm. If you tie them like the diagram, cut two each that are 20 in/ 50cm. Knot your strings and secure.

2. Select a color to start with, and hold the remaining strings in your hand in a bunch. Make a LEFT LOOP KNOT over all of the strings and pull it up tightly to the top of your bracelet.

3. Continue making LEFT LOOP KNOTS until you would like to switch colors. The knots will spiral around the bracelet as you are knotting. You will need to pass the string around the back of the bracelet after you have made about eight knots so that it continues to spiral properly.

4. When you wish to switch colors, select a thread that is closest to the knot that you just completed. When you make the next knot, it will sit close to the previous one and not leave a gap. Make sure you add the old color of strings to the group of strings you are knotting around.

5. When you have knotted your bracelet to the correct length, tie the strings in a knot at the bottom, and if you like, you can braid the ends.

The Criss Cross

This bracelet is a variation of the Simple Stripes bracelet on page 24. This time, you will use a LEFT LOOP KNOT and a RIGHT LOOP KNOT. You may find it easier to use the colors shown below the first time so you can match the steps exactly, and then select your own colors when you understand the pattern.

🔵 72 in/180 cm
1 per color

🔺 36 in/90 cm
2 per color

1. Cut your threads according to the chart measurements and knot them. Tie a knot at the top and tape the knot to your work surface.

2. Using the left-most string (string 1) tie a RIGHT LOOP KNOT over string 2, string 3, string 4, string 5 and then string 6.

3. Repeat this step with the remaining five colors, always working from the left to the right.

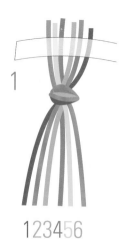

1

123456

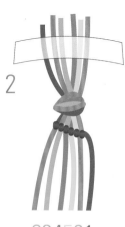

2

234561

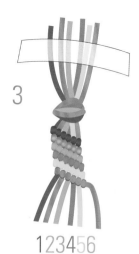

3

123456

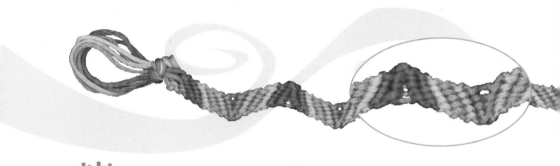

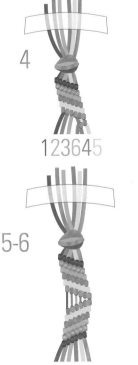

4

123645

5-6

123456

4. Now you are going to do the reverse of this to create the return pattern. Pick up string 6, which is back on the right side, and make a LEFT LOOP KNOT on string 5.

5. Carry on knotting string 6 with left loop knots on strings 4, 3, 2 and 1. It should now be on the left side of the bracelet.

6. Carry on with knotting, picking up the strings from the right and knotting back to the left until you have knotted all six colors.

7. Repeat steps 2 through 6, knotting left and then right with each of the strings until you are finished your bracelet. Tie it off and give with pride!

Variation: Add a bead on the end strings each time you reverse the knotting. This creates a whole new look! Use beads that are large enough to thread, but not so large as to be awkward. Size E seed beads work well.

Cupid's Arrow

This is a popular bracelet and looks great with anything you wear. It is similar to the Criss Cross, so if you have made that bracelet first, you will have no problems with this one. Instead of knotting across all the strings in one direction, you will knot across half the strings in one direction and then the other half of the strings in the other direction. This creates the "V" or chevron design of the bracelet.

| | 60 in/150 cm 1 per color | | 30 in/80 cm 2 per color |

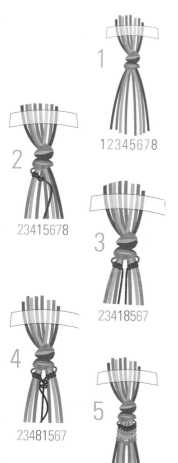

1 12345678

2 23415678

3 23418567

4 23481567

5 87654321

1. Choose four colors of thread and cut the appropriate lengths. Knot them together at the top and tape onto your work surface.

2. Start with string 8 and LEFT LOOP KNOT over strings 7, 6 and 5, finishing in the middle position.

3. Now pick up string 1 and RIGHT LOOP KNOT over strings 2, 3 and 4, finishing beside string 8.

4. LEFT LOOP KNOT string 8 and string 1 together. You now have completed one arrow!

5. Repeat step two using string 7, and knotting over the three strings to the right.

6. Repeat step three using string 2, and knotting over the three strings to the left.

7. Knots strings 2 and 7 together to make your second arrow.

8. Continue this pattern of working from the left over three strings, and then the right over three strings and finishing with a center knot until your bracelet is finished.

The Ladder

This bracelet is next in the book because it uses a combination of the wrapping and knotting techniques from the Swirls that you just made on page 29 and the straight knotting that you did to make Cupid's Arrow page 33. If you know how to make both of these bracelets, then even though this one looks quite tricky, you will find it a snap to make!

1

12345678

56 in/140 cm
1 per color

28 in/70 cm
2 per color

1. Cut four colors of threads. Knot them at the top and attach to your work surface.

2. Follow the instructions on page 33 for the Cupid's Arrow, knotting RIGHT LOOP KNOTS with String 1 from the left and then LEFT LOOP KNOTS from the right with String 8 to create a chevron. (Remember that "chevron" is the word used to describe a wide V shape.) Don't forget to knot strings 1 and 8 in the middle to make the point of the chevron.

3. Repeat this with each of the threads until you have created a chevron with each color.

4. Once you have knotted four chevrons, split the strings into two groups, making sure you have one of each color in each group.

2-4

12345678

5-6

8

2 3 4 1   5 6 7

5. Now you are going to use the same instructions as you used to make the Swirl Bracelet on page 29. Choose one color of thread from the group on the left, and start to make LEFT LOOP KNOTS over the remaining three threads in that group of strings. Make ten knots with the left group of strings.

6. Now using the same color from the right group of strings, make TEN RIGHT LOOP KNOTS over the remaining threads in that group of strings.

7. Now spread your strings back out in the same order as they are in the diagram.

8. Repeat steps 2 through 7 until you have the length of bracelet you wish, and then tie the threads in a knot to finish it.

7

2 3 4 1 8 5 6 7

Hint: This is a great bracelet to add beads to. Slide the bead over the thread that you are using to knot the Swirl section of the pattern, right before you switch back to the Cupid's Arrow pattern. It looks really cool!

Patchwork Stripes

This funky bracelet uses exactly the same techniques as the Simple Stripes, but by changing the order of the strings that you knot over, you get a completely different look! This is a bright, colorful bracelet made from six strands, but you can experiment and see what it would look like with eight strands, or even try ten for a different effect.

The trick to this bracelet is to be able to work the strings in a forwards and backwards order. It is really quite simple to do and creates a great pattern. Try it with colors that are similar to each other to create a totally different look.

	64 in/160 cm		32 in/80 cm
	1 per color		2 per color

For an six color, six strand bracelet:

1. Select six colors and cut 32 inch/80 cm lengths of each color. Knot them at the top and tape them to your work surface.

2. Instead of starting with the end thread, we are going to start with the thread second from the right- string 5.
Pick up string 5 and make a RIGHT LOOP KNOT over string 6.
Look at the new order of the strings — string 5 and string 6 have now reversed position.

3. Work backwards now by picking up string 4. Tie RIGHT LOOP KNOTS over string 6 and string 5.

1 2 3 4 5 6

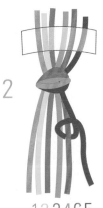

2

1 2 3 4 6 5

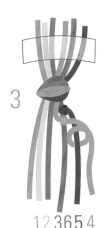

3

1 2 3 6 5 4

4. Now pick up string 3 and tie RIGHT LOOP KNOTS over strings 6, 5 and 4. Can you start to see the pattern? You are picking up the strings in a reverse order, but still knotting forward.

5. Pick up string 2 and tie RIGHT LOOP KNOTS over strings 6, 5, 4 and 3.

6. Pick up string 1 and tie RIGHT LOOP KNOTS over strings 6, 5, 4, 3 and 2.

1 2 6 5 4 3

1 6 5 4 3 2

6 5 4 3 2 1

Now, look at the order of your threads, they have completely reversed! String 6 is now on the left, and string 1 is on the right. Guess what the next part of the pattern is?

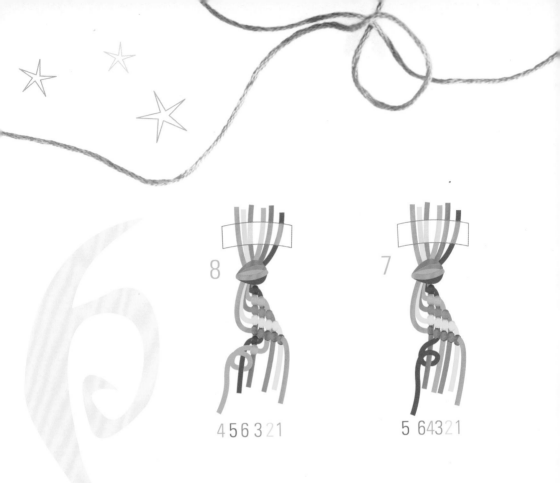

8   7

4 5 6 3 2 1   5 6 4 3 2 1

7. Pick up string 5 and tie a LEFT LOOP KNOT over string 6.

8. Pick up string 4 and tie a LEFT LOOP KNOT over string 6 and 5.

Also: As you finish this bracelet, you will notice that you are now starting to use more of one color in a bracelet than others. So make sure you cut them long enough initially and trim the ends when you are done so they are even.

9. Pick up string 3 and tie LEFT LOOP KNOTS over strings 6, 5 and 4.

10. Pick up string 2 and tie LEFT LOOP KNOTS over strings 6, 5, 4 and 3.

11. Pick up string 1 and tie LEFT LOOP KNOTS over strings 6, 5, 4, 3 and 2.

9

3 4 5 6 2 1

10

2 3 4 5 6 1

11

1 2 3 4 5 6

You are now back to the beginning of the pattern. Start again at step 2, and repeat each step until you have tied a bracelet that is the correct length for you. Knot the threads at the end and tie on your wrist!

Diamond Weave

This is a more complicated bracelet to make, but with such a pretty pattern it is worth the time it takes to master it! Your friends will be thrilled to receive this bracelet, so go slowly and pay attention to the order of the forward and backward knots, as well as to your place in the pattern. You can do it!

 40 in/100 cm   20 in/50 cm

1. The first thing to do is to lay out your strings in the proper order, as shown in the diagram. We suggest you use the same colors we do the first time so that you are able to learn the pattern more easily.

2. The first four rows of knots will be chevrons, as you did in Cupid's Arrow on page 33. Remember how this goes? Start with string 1 and tie RIGHT LOOP KNOTS over strings 2, 3 and 4.

3. Pick up string 8 and tie LEFT LOOP KNOTS over strings 7, 6 and 5.

4. Tie a RIGHT LOOP KNOT with strings 1 and 8 which are now in the center.

5. Go ahead and continue with strings 2 and 7, 3 and 6 and 4 and 5 until you have four chevrons.

6. Now you are going to tie the knots that create the red knot at the side of the large "X" shape.

7

21345687

8-9

4 213 6875

7. With strings 1 and 2, tie a RIGHT LOOP KNOT. Then with strings 7 and 8, tie a LEFT LOOP KNOT.

8. Next you are going to start knotting the bottom half of the "X", and the reverse chevrons. With string 4, LEFT LOOP KNOT over string 3, 1 and 2.

9. With string 5, RIGHT LOOP KNOT over string 6, 8 and 7.

10. With string 3, tie RIGHT LOOP KNOTS over strings 6, 8, 7 and 5.

11. With string 6, tie LEFT LOOP KNOTS over 1, 2 and 4.

12. With string 1, tie RIGHT LOOP KNOTS over string 8, 7, 5 and 6.

13. With string 8, tie LEFT LOOP KNOTS over string 2, 4, and 6. Then with string 2, tie RIGHT LOOP KNOTS over string 7, 5, and 3. Continue to knot the two sets of red strings until you see a mirror image of the top half.

10-11

64218753

12-13

78645312

14-15

78536412

16

78563412

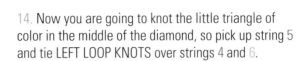

14. Now you are going to knot the little triangle of color in the middle of the diamond, so pick up string 5 and tie LEFT LOOP KNOTS over strings 4 and 6.

15. With string 4, tie a RIGHT LOOP KNOT over string 3.

16. With string 3 and 6, tie a RIGHT LOOP KNOT to create the spot in the center of the triangle. Continue to create the chevron pattern, starting from step 2.

You have now completed the entire pattern! This section is shown in detail in the photograph to the (right). You are now going to repeat this entire pattern until you have a bracelet long enough for your wrist. So go back to step 2, and repeat step 2 through 16 until your bracelet is long enough, and then knot it and give it to someone special.

Southern Trinidad

This adapted V pattern looks easier than the Diamond Weave, but don't be deceived! If you master the Diamond Weave pattern first, this one will be a snap. On this bracelet you will see that you knot the middle strings first, and then the outer edges. Then you move back to the middle strings. So you aren't working in a row the way you have previously. The results look great though, and the colors are pretty; it's one of our favorite bracelets in the book! Be patient and have fun making the Southern Trinidad.

12345678

2-3

12536478

4-5

25136847

64 in/160 cm
1 per color

32 in/80 cm
2 per color

1. Cut and knot your strings, lay them out in the same order by color as we do.

2. Start with the center "v" by picking up string 4 and tying a RIGHT LOOP KNOT over string 5, and then string 6.

3. With string 5, tie a LEFT LOOP KNOT over string 3.

4. Now you are moving to the left edge and must use string 1 to tie a RIGHT LOOP KNOT over string 2 and 5.

5. Now to the right edge and use string 8 to tie a LEFT LOOP KNOT over string 7 and 4.

Check your string order, it should be 25136847.

6-7

25618347

6. Now back to the center. String 3 RIGHT LOOP KNOTS over string 6 and 8.

7. Use string 6 to tie a LEFT LOOP KNOT over string 1.

8. Back to the left side. String 2 RIGHT LOOP KNOTS over 5 and 6.

9. On the right side, string 7 LEFT LOOP KNOTS over string 4 and 3. (56218734) Again, check your string order to help you stay on track.

10. In the center, string 1 RIGHT LOOP KNOTS over string 8 and 7.

11. String 8 LEFT LOOP KNOTS over string 2.

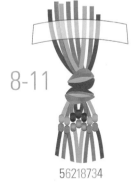

8-11

56218734

12-13

68527413

12. On the left, string 5 RIGHT LOOP KNOTS over string 6 and string 8.

13. On the right, string 4 LEFT LOOP KNOTS over strings 3 and 1.

14. Back the center use string 2 to tie RIGHT LOOP KNOTS over strings 7 and 4.

15. Use string 7 to tie a LEFT LOOP KNOT over string 5.

16. On the left, string 6 RIGHT LOOP KNOTS over strings 8 and 7.

17. On the right, string 3 LEFT LOOP KNOTS over strings 1 and 2 (87654321). Check your ending string order to make sure you are on track.

14-17

87654321

You have just completed the entire pattern! Did you notice that your strings have ended up in the reverse order of how you started? Because this bracelet has two of each color, you won't see a difference when you repeat the pattern. If you used six different colors though, when you repeat the pattern, the order of the colors will be reversed.

Why don't you try six colors with your next bracelet to see how pretty the results are?

Trinidad

Up until now, all of the knotted, flat bracelets were made by placing a knot on every string in every row. With the Trinidad bracelet however, we start using the technique of skipping knots. This creates the almost "lacey" effect in the bracelet and is very elegant. Use two colors that are quite different from each other the first time so that you can see what you are doing more clearly.

1

12345678

60 in/150 cm
2 per color

30 in/75 cm
4 per color

1. Cut your strings, knot them at the top and tape the knot to your work surface. Arrange your threads as shown, with four strands of one color in the middle, and two strands each of the second color on each side.

2. Start by working on the edges. Use string 1 and make a RIGHT LOOP KNOT over string 2 and string 3.

3. Use string 8 to make a LEFT LOOP KNOT over string 7 and 6.

4. Now use string 3 to make a RIGHT LOOP KNOT over string 1 and 4.

5. Use string 6 to make a LEFT LOOP KNOT over string 8 and 5. (21436587)

6. Use string 3 to make a RIGHT LOOP KNOT over string 6 to complete the chevron.

2-3

23145867

4-6

21463587

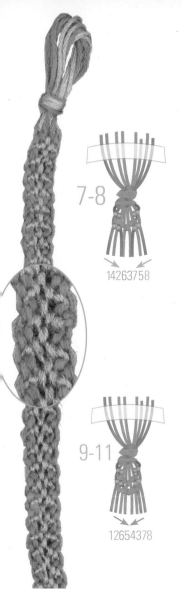

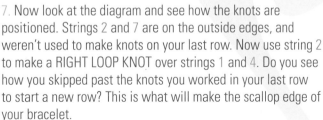

7-8

14263758

7. Now look at the diagram and see how the knots are positioned. Strings 2 and 7 are on the outside edges, and weren't used to make knots on your last row. Now use string 2 to make a RIGHT LOOP KNOT over strings 1 and 4. Do you see how you skipped past the knots you worked in your last row to start a new row? This is what will make the scallop edge of your bracelet.

8. Use string 7 to make a LEFT LOOP KNOT over strings 8 and 5.

9. Move to the inside and pick up string 4 and make RIGHT LOOP KNOTS over strings 2 and 6. (12643758)

10. Use string 5 to make LEFT LOOP KNOTS over strings 7 and 3. (12645378)

9-11

11. Now use string 4 to make a RIGHT LOOP KNOT over string 5.

Repeat the pattern from step 2 to 11 until your bracelet is long enough and tie off with a knot.

12654378

Hint: Tension refers to how tightly or how loosely the threads are knotted. Until now, it hasn't been terribly important. With this bracelet, however, you will want to pay attention to this, and try to keep the knots consistent — not too tight, not too loose, in order to create an even pattern. Try this bracelet using four different colors — two strands of each and see what the effect is.

Super Stripes

Super Stripes bracelet is a lot like the very first one you did; Simple Stripes — in that all of the knots move in one direction only. So choose which direction you would like to knot in; we choose to do LEFT LOOP KNOTS for this bracelet, but it works just as well with RIGHT LOOP KNOTS.

60 in/150 cm 1 per color	32 in/80 cm 2 per color

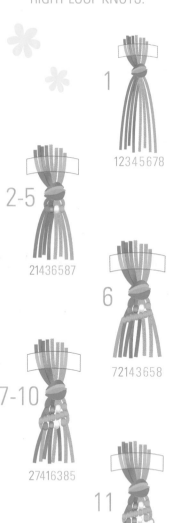

1. Cut and knot your threads. Arrange the threads in the same order we have them — each color side by side.

2. With 7 and 8, tie a LEFT LOOP KNOT.

3. With strings 5 and 6, tie a LEFT LOOP KNOT.

4. With strings 3 and 4, tie a LEFT LOOP KNOT.

5. With strings 1 and 2, tie a LEFT LOOP KNOT.

6. Now, start with string 7, and the right end, and tie LEFT LOOP KNOTS all the way across — on string 8, 5, 6, 3, 4, 1 and 2.

7. With string 8, tie a LEFT LOOP KNOT over string 5.

8. With string 6, tie a LEFT LOOP KNOT over string 3.

9. With string 4, tie a LEFT LOOP KNOT over string 1.

10. With string 2, tie a LEFT LOOP KNOT over string 7.

11. Now go back to the right side and use string 5 to tie a LEFT LOOP KNOT over string 8, 3, 6, 1, 4, 7 and 2.

How easy is this? I'll bet you thought it would be tough, but we threw an easy one in here because we thought you would like a break from the tough bracelets. Good job, and have fun repeating this pattern until your bracelet is finished. Happy knotting!

Eternity Bracelet

This is such a great bracelet! It looks fantastic on, and is a wonderful gift to give and receive. It is one of the more time consuming bracelets in the book, but with the skills you have gained up to this point you should be able to master this one before too long. You will work this one almost as two separate bracelets, only meeting in the middle to connect and cross over. Although there are a lot of steps, don't worry; it is just because you have to work each side separately. You repeat the same pattern, though, so it is quite simple really.

12345678

68 in/175 cm	34 in/85 cm
1 per color	2 per color

1. Cut, knot and tape your threads to your work surface. Arrange the threads so that two colors are on one side, and two colors are on the other side.

2. You are going to start knotting chevrons, but you are not going to tie the center knot. This keeps the two parts of the bracelet separate. So start with string 1 and tie RIGHT LOOP KNOTS over strings 2, 3 and 4.

3. With string 8, tie LEFT LOOP KNOTS over strings 7, 6 and 5.

2-3

23418567

4-9

12345678

10

12354678

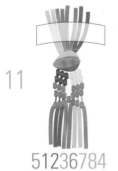

11

51236784

4. With string 2 tie RIGHT LOOP KNOTS over strings 3, 4 and 1.

5. With string 7, tie LEFT LOOP KNOTS over strings 6, 5 and 8.

6. With string 3, tie RIGHT LOOP KNOT over strings 4, 1 and 2.

7. With string 6, tie LEFT LOOP KNOTS over strings 5, 8 and 7.

8. With string 4, tie RIGHT LOOP KNOTS over strings 1, 2 and 3.

9. With String 5, tie LEFT LOOP KNOTS over strings 8, 7 and 6
Your string order is now as it was in the beginning: 1, 2, 3, 4,5,
6 ,7 ,8.

10. You have half the loop done, and now you are going to join
them together in the middle and cross over. Take string 4 and
tie a RIGHT LOOP KNOT over string 5.

11. Then continue with string 4 knotting over strings 6, 7, and 8.
Take string 5 and LEFT LOOP KNOT over 3, 2, and 1.

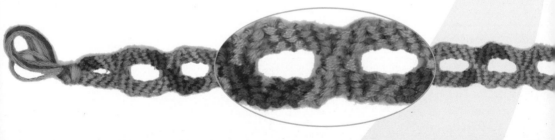

12. Now reverse the chevron pattern for two rows. With string 3, RIGHT LOOP KNOT over strings 6, 7, 8, and 4. (51236784)

12-13

65127843

13. With string 6, LEFT LOOP KNOT over string 2, 1 and 5.

14. Now start the half chevron pattern again that you started with this time with your colors on the opposite sides of your bracelet. With string 6, RIGHT LOOP KNOT over strings 5, 1 and 2.

15. With string 3, LEFT LOOP KNOT over string 4, 8 and 7.

16. With string 5, RIGHT LOOP KNOT over string 1, 2 and 6.

14-17

12654378

17. With string 4, LEFT LOOP KNOT over string 8, 7 and 3.

18. With string 1, RIGHT LOOP KNOT over string 2, 6 and 5.

19. With string 8, LEFT LOOP KNOT over string 7, 3 and 4.

20. With string 2, RIGHT LOOP KNOT over string 6, 5 and 1.

21. With string 7, LEFT LOOP KNOT over string 3, 4 and 8.

22. Now refer back to step 10 and continue to knot your eternity bracelet, by joining the two sides in the center.

18-21

65127843

22a

65178432

22b

76518432

To Finish: You have now completed the separate sides and you are going to join the loop again. So start with step 10 and follow the pattern through to the end. Repeat steps 10 to 22 until you have a bracelet long enough to wear.

The Zipper

We decided to put this bracelet in the book as a final challenge. It looks deceptively easy, but uses an entirely different style of knotting to create the zipper tooth effect. To make your first bracelet, we recommend using two colors that contrast in order to see how it is going along as you knot. Pay attention to the "**overs**" and "**unders**" in order to get the right effect, and also to the tension so that the pattern remains even.

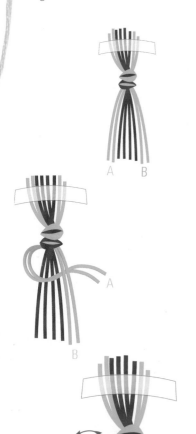

1. Choose two colors of threads and cut four pieces of each — about 12 inches/ 30cm long for the center color, and 24 inches/ 60 cm long for the outer colors. Knot the strings and tape them to your work surface.

2. Arrange the shorter threads in the center and two of the longer threads on each side. Pick up the two strands on the left (A) and cross them **over** the strings in the center leaving a bit of a loop on the left and pass it **under** strands B. (almost like the shape of a "4")

3. Now pick up strands B and pass them **under** strands A and the center strands, and pull them **up** through the loop on the left side. Pull the knot tight, sliding it up to the top.

4. Strands A and B have now switched sides. Take strands B, and pass them **under** the center strands and **over** strands A.

5. Take strands A and pass them **over** the center strands and **down** through the loop and pull the knot tight, sliding it to the top.

That is it! It seems easy, but requires you to pay attention to the directions. Keep knotting until your bracelet is finished, and then tie it off.

Record Log

We hope that you continue to enjoy creating friendship bracelets and giving them to people you care about. They are a wonderful way to tell your friends that you think they are special and that they are worth the work you did to make these beautiful tokens!

These final few pages are a place where you can keep track of the bracelets you create, when you created them, who you gave them to and when.

Bracelet _____

Made By _____

Given To _____

Date _____

Notes _____

Bracelet _____

Made By _____

Given To _____

Date _____

Notes _____

Bracelet _____

Made By _____

Given To _____

Date _____

Notes _____

_____

Bracelet _____

Made By _____

Given To _____

Date _____

Notes _____

_____

Bracelet _____

Made By _____

Given To _____

Date _____

Notes _____

_____

inches

0

1

2

3

4

5

6

cm

— 0

— 1

— 2

— 3

— 4

— 5

— 6

— 7

— 8

— 9

— 10

— 11

— 12

— 13

— 14

— 15

— 16

— 17

Bracelet _____

Made By _____

Given To _____

Date _____

Notes _____

_____

Bracelet _____

Made By _____

Given To _____

Date _____

Notes _____

_____

Bracelet _____

Made By _____

Given To _____

Date _____

Notes _____

_____

Bracelet _____

Made By _____

Given To _____

Date _____

Notes _____

_____

Bracelet _____

Made By _____

Given To _____

Date _____

Notes _____

_____

Bracelet _____

Made By _____

Given To _____

Date _____

Notes _____

_____

inches

0

1

2

3

4

5

6

cm
0
1
2
3
4
5
6
7
8
9
10
11
12
13
14
15
16
17

Bracelet _____

Made By _____

Given To _____

Date _____

Notes _____

_____

Bracelet _____

Made By _____

Given To _____

Date _____

Notes _____

_____

Bracelet _____

Made By _____

Given To _____

Date _____

Notes _____

_____

Bracelet _____

Made By _____

Given To _____

Date _____

Notes _____

_____

Bracelet _____

Made By _____

Given To _____

Date _____

Notes _____

_____

Bracelet _____

Made By _____

Given To _____

Date _____

Notes _____

_____

inches

0

1

2

3

4

5

6

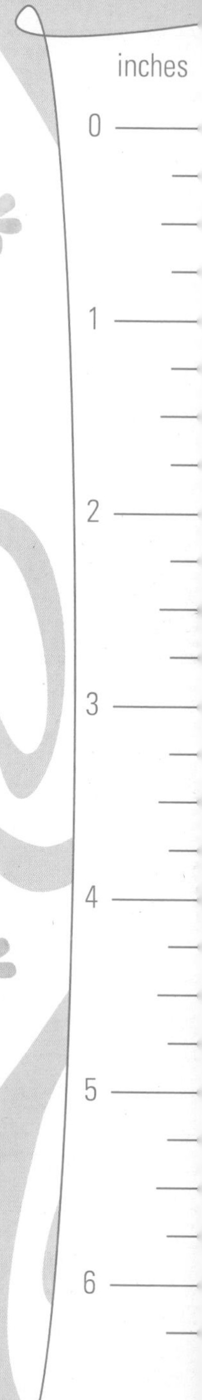